TRY NOT TO LAUGH
Easter Challenge

EASTER JOKE BOOK FOR KIDS

Instructions

The Rules are Simple:

Pick your team, or go one on one.

Sit across from each other & make eye contact.

Take turns reading jokes to each other.

You can make silly faces, funny sound effects, etc.

When your opponent laughs, you get a point!

First team to win 3 points, WINS!

WIN

If You're Laughing, You're Losing!

Easter Egg Hunt

Hidden in this book are Eggs that looks like this.

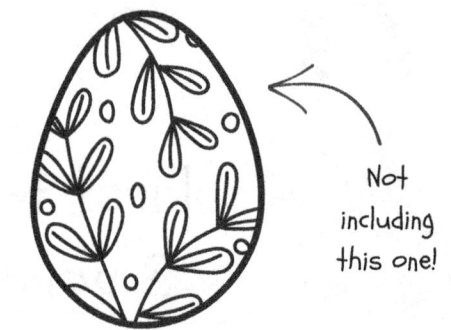

Not including this one!

How many times can you find this egg inside this book?

Answer at the back

What did the egg say after a good workout?

Omelette stronger now!

What kind of egg lives at the North Pole?

An egg-loo!

What do you call a rabbit who works in a barbershop?

A hare stylist!

Who tells the funniest egg jokes?

Comedi-hens!

Where do tough chickens come from?

Hard-boiled eggs!

What kind of shoes did the frog wear at Easter?

Open toad sandals!

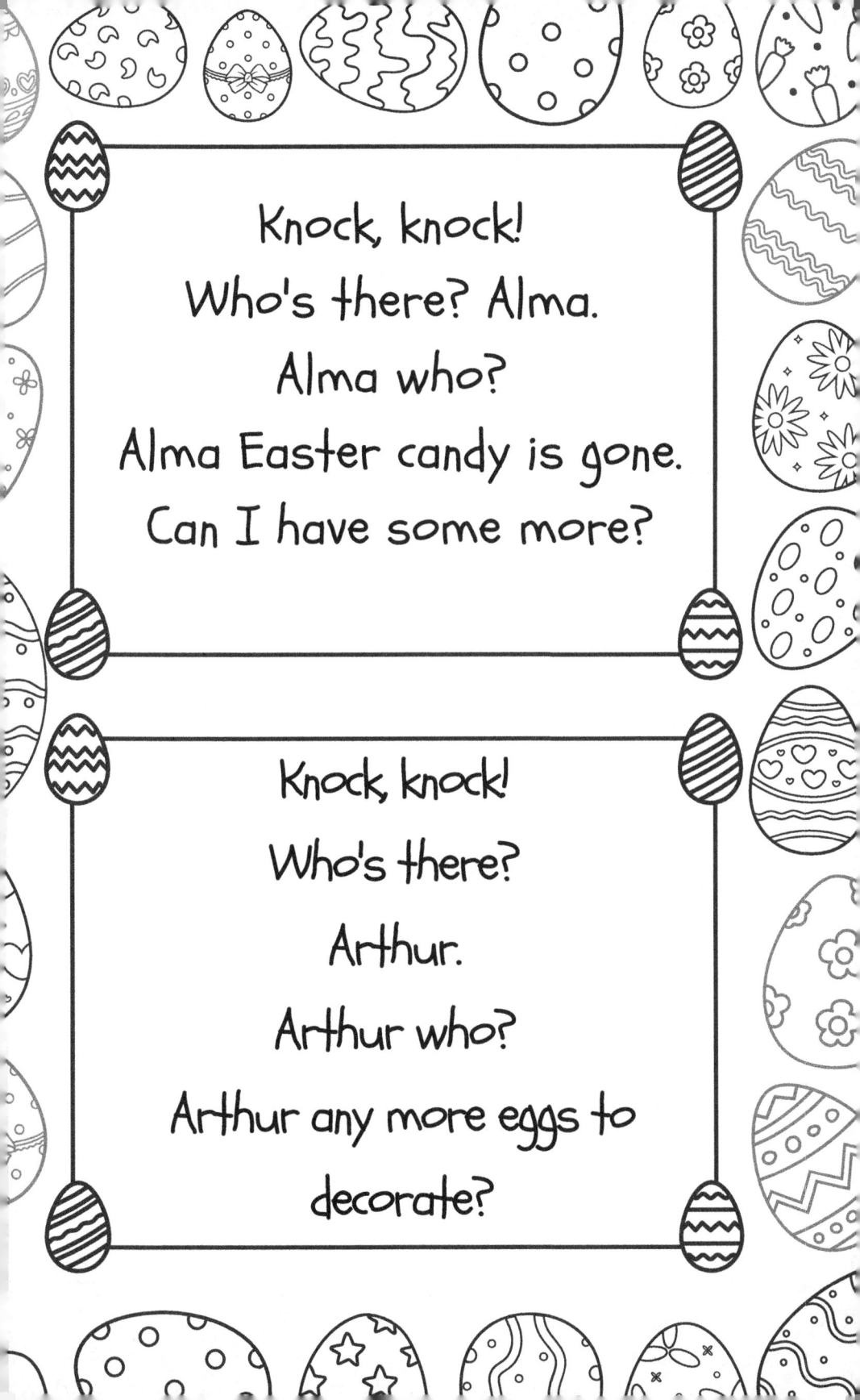

Knock, knock!
Who's there? Alma.
Alma who?
Alma Easter candy is gone.
Can I have some more?

Knock, knock!
Who's there?
Arthur.
Arthur who?
Arthur any more eggs to decorate?

What do you call a mischievous Easter egg?

A practical yolker!

What's the Easter Bunny's favorite music?

Hip-hop!

Why don't bunnies get hot in the summer?

Because they have hare-conditioning!

Which petrol station do eggs use?

Shell!

How does a chicken prefer to pay for their shopping?

By using the eggs-press checkout!

What did the egg say about escaping the chef?

"I might whisk it and run!"

What's the best way to catch a squirrel in spring?

Climb a tree and act like a nut!

What did the big flower say to the little flower?

Hi, bud!

What do you call a rabbit who loves adventure?

A hare-dventurer!

What do you call a zen Easter egg?

An ommmmmmlet.

Why did Humpty Dumpty have a great fall?

To make up for his miserable summer.

Why are you so tired in April?

Because you just finished a March.

What kind of stories do Easter eggs tell?

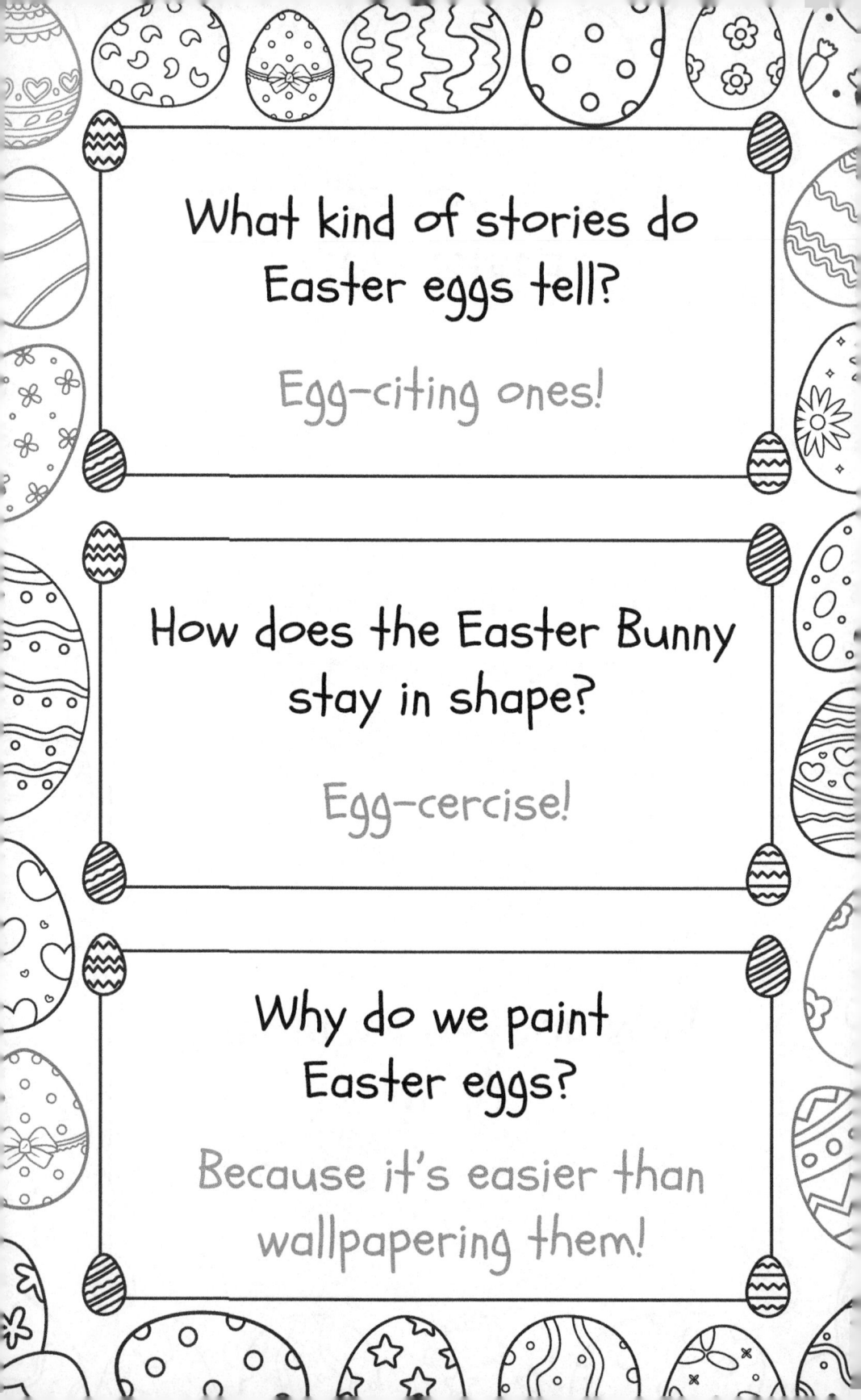

Egg-citing ones!

How does the Easter Bunny stay in shape?

Egg-cercise!

Why do we paint Easter eggs?

Because it's easier than wallpapering them!

Why don't Easter eggs tell jokes?

Because they might crack up!

What do you call a rabbit who tells good jokes?

A funny bunny!

Why did the Easter Bunny cross the road?

To prove he wasn't chicken!

One Easter, Tommy, proudly announced he was giving up chocolate for Lent. Impressive for a six-year-old—until we caught him sneaking chocolate eggs from his own basket.

"Tommy!" I said. "I thought you gave up chocolate!"
Without missing a beat, he stuffed another egg in his mouth and mumbled, "I did. But the Easter Bunny didn't remember that I had, so this doesn't count!"
We couldn't argue with his logic. Now, every Easter, "Easter Bunny Loopholes" are an official family tradition!

Knock, knock.
Who's there?
Don't Butcher.
Don't Butcher who?
Don't Butcher all your eggs in one basket!

Knock, knock
Who's there?
Elf.
Elf who?
Elf me find all the Easter eggs!

What's a bunny's favorite restaurant?

IHOP!

Why did the Easter egg hide?

Because it was a little chicken!

How do rabbits travel?

By hare-plane!

What do you get if you cross a rabbit with a spider?

A hare-net!

How do you know if a rabbit's been in your fridge?

There are 24 carrot marks!

What's a bunny's favorite dance move?

The bunny hop!

What do you get when you pour hot water down a rabbit hole?

A hot cross bunny!

Why was the Easter Bunny so sad?

He was having a bad hare day!

Why do eggs like to go to school?

So they can be egg-ucated!

What do you call a bunny who tells tall tales?

A hare-raiser!

How does the Easter Bunny stay organized?

He writes everything in a hare-planner!

Why did the chick join the band?

Because it had the drumsticks!

What do you call a sleepy Easter egg?

Egg-zosted!

What do rabbits say before they eat?

Lettuce pray!

What do you call an Easter egg from outer space?

An egg-straterrestrial!

How did the Easter Bunny fix his fur?

With a harebrush!

What's a rabbit's favorite sport?

Basket-ball!

Why was the little chick so good at baseball?

Because it had a great peep-er arm!

What do you call a bunny magician?

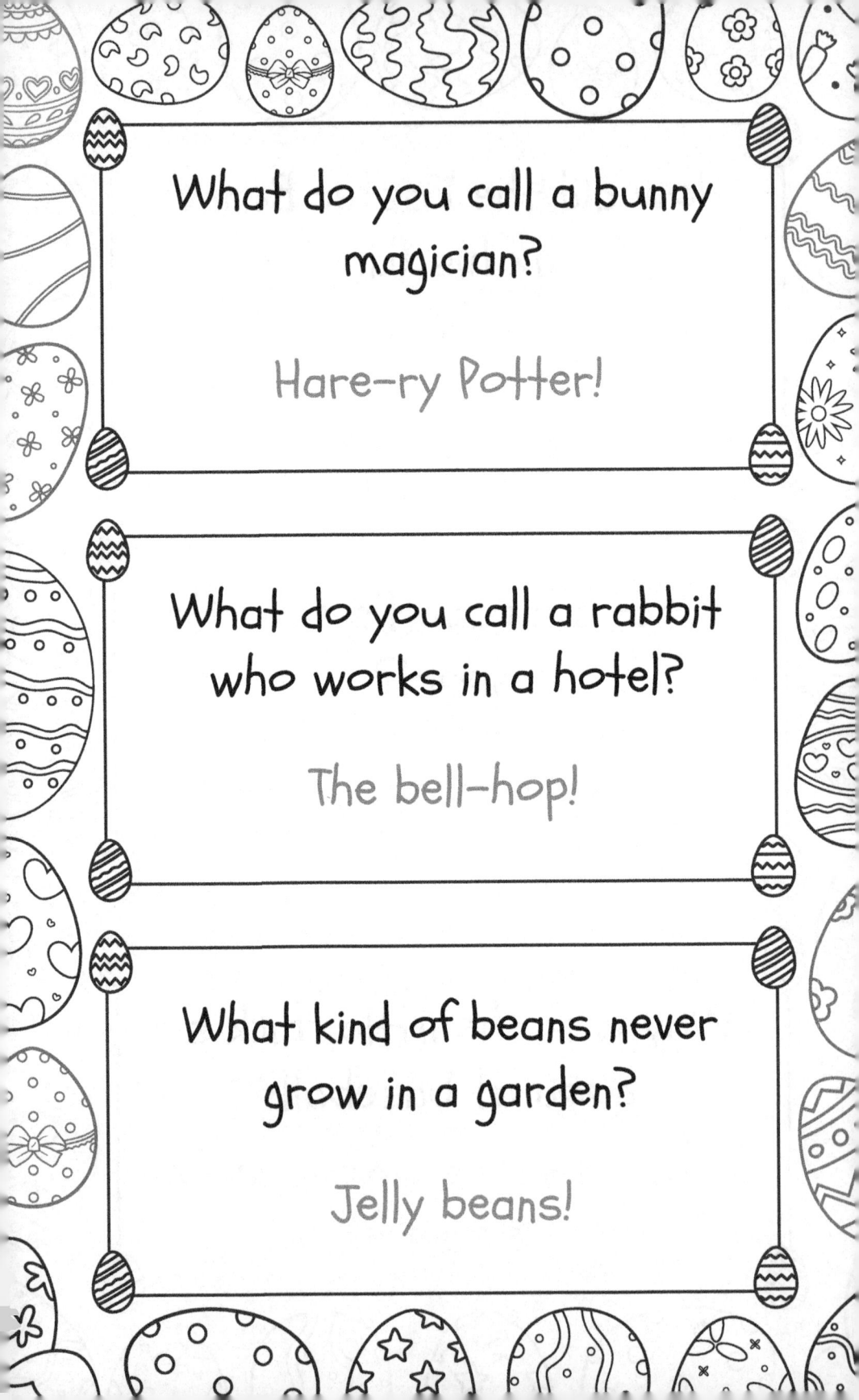

Hare-ry Potter!

What do you call a rabbit who works in a hotel?

The bell-hop!

What kind of beans never grow in a garden?

Jelly beans!

What's the best way to make Easter easier?

Put an "i" where the "t" is!

What do you call a chocolate bunny that lays eggs?

A choco-doodle-doo!

What do you get when you cross a bumblebee with a bunny?

A honey bunny!

Knock, knock.
Who's there?
Howard.
Howard who?
Howard you like some nice Easter eggs?

Knock, knock
Who's there?
Leaf.
Leaf who?
Leaf me some treats this Easter!

What did the Easter egg ask for at the hair salon?

A new dye job!

What do rabbits say when they come home from work?

"Anybunny home?"

What's an egg's favorite American Football team?

Chick-ago Bears!

What do you call an Easter Bunny who gets kicked out of school?

Egg-spelled.

Did you hear about the bunny who sat on a bumblebee?

It's a tender tail!

What do Easter chicks have to do before they can become hens?

Pass their eggs-ams.

What's a rabbit's favorite type of workout?

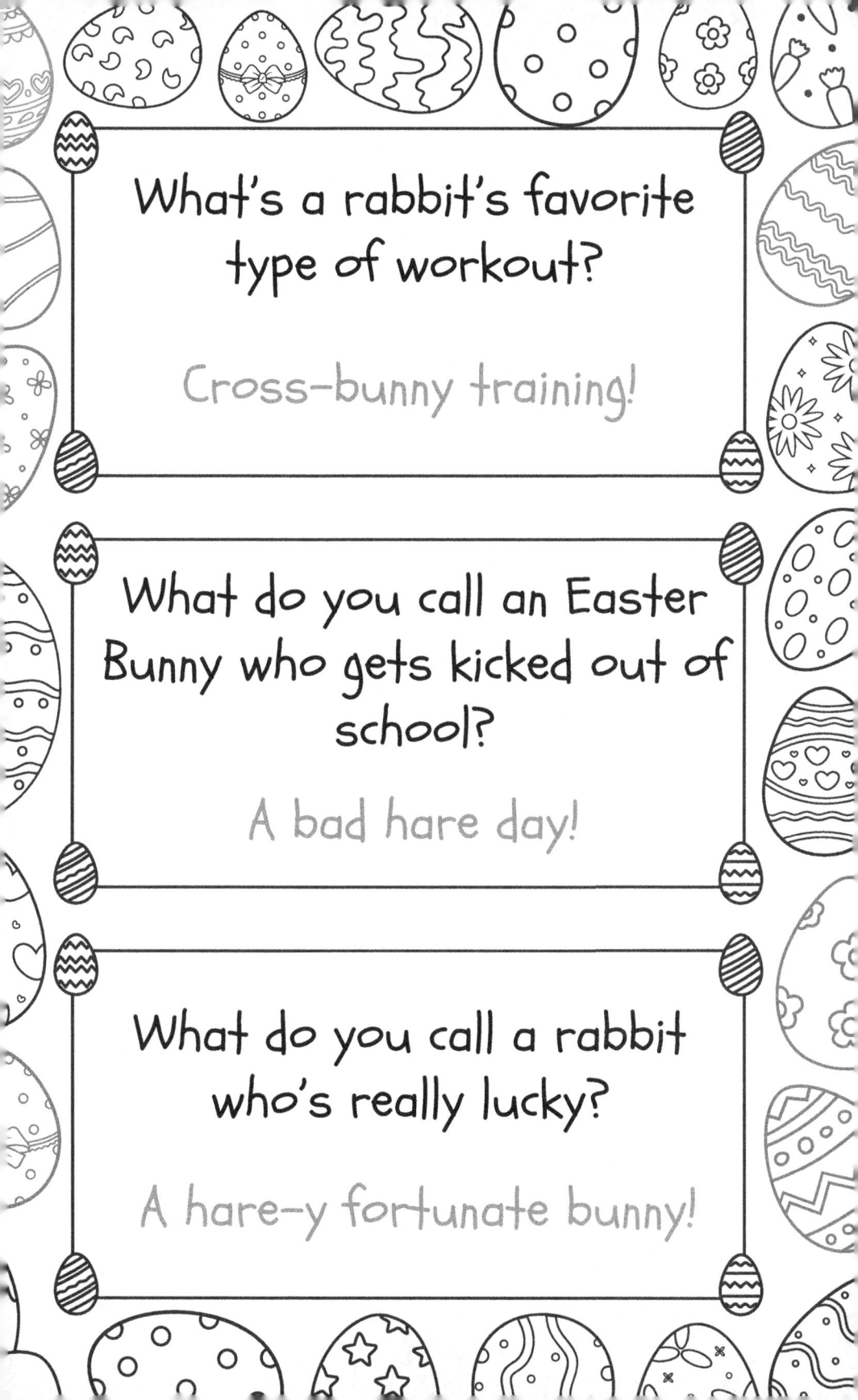

Cross-bunny training!

What do you call an Easter Bunny who gets kicked out of school?

A bad hare day!

What do you call a rabbit who's really lucky?

A hare-y fortunate bunny!

Why did the Easter Bunny bring a ladder?

Because he wanted to go to new heights!

What did the egg say after telling a joke?

"Was that egg-citing or what?"

Why did the chocolate bunny go to therapy?

Because he felt so hollow inside!

What did the bunny say to the carrot?

It's been nice gnawing you!

What kind of bedtime stories do baby bunnies like?

Hare-y tales!

What do you get if you cross a rabbit with a frog?

A bunny ribbit!

What's an Easter egg's least favorite day of the week?

Fry-day!

What do you get when you cross a rabbit with an owl?

A hare who gives a hoot!

What kind of stories do Easter eggs like to tell?

Yolk tales!

What do you call an Easter Bunny with fleas?

Bugs Bunny!

Why was the Easter Bunny so good at math?

Because he could multiply!

What's the Easter Bunny's favorite type of jewelry?

24-carrot gold!

What do you call a bunny who tells lies?

A little fib-hopper!

What do you get when you cross an Easter egg with a comedian?

Egg-stra laughs!

Why don't rabbits get cold in the winter?

Because they have fur-tastic coats!

Knock, knock.
Who's there?
Bunny.
Bunny who?
Bunny of your business!

Knock, knock.
Who's there?
Lettuce.
Lettuce who?
Lettuce in, it's Easter!

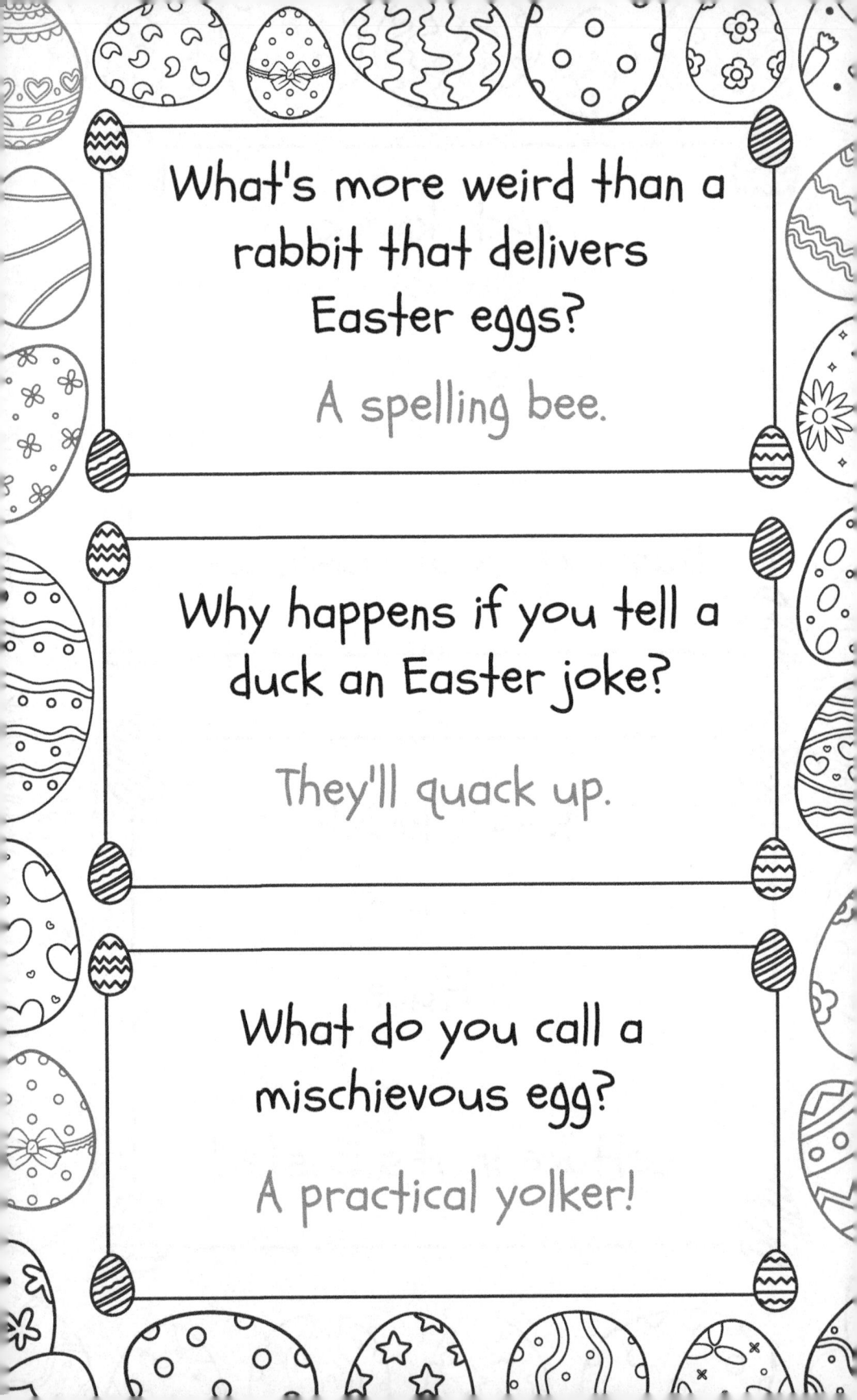

What's more weird than a rabbit that delivers Easter eggs?

A spelling bee.

Why happens if you tell a duck an Easter joke?

They'll quack up.

What do you call a mischievous egg?

A practical yolker!

Knock, knock!
Who's there?
Donna.
Donna who?
Donna want to decorate some eggs?

Knock, knock!
Who's there?
Harvey.
Harvey who?
Harvey good Easter everyone.

Where do Easter Bunnies go for new tails?

To the retail store.

What does the bunny say about the 'soup-of-the-day' he serves at his restaurant?

It's egg-stra special.

Why did the rabbit go to the hair salon?

She found a few too many gray hares!

Knock, knock.
Who's there?
Chick.
Chick who?
Chick out my Easter basket!

Knock, knock
Who's there?
Peter.
Peter who?
Peter Cottontail, ready for Easter!

What do you call a line of rabbits walking backward?

A receding hare-line!

Why did the Easter Bunny bring a ladder to the party?

Because he heard the drinks were on the house!

Did you hear about the egg who went to therapy?

It had shell shock!

What do you call a rabbit who won the lottery?

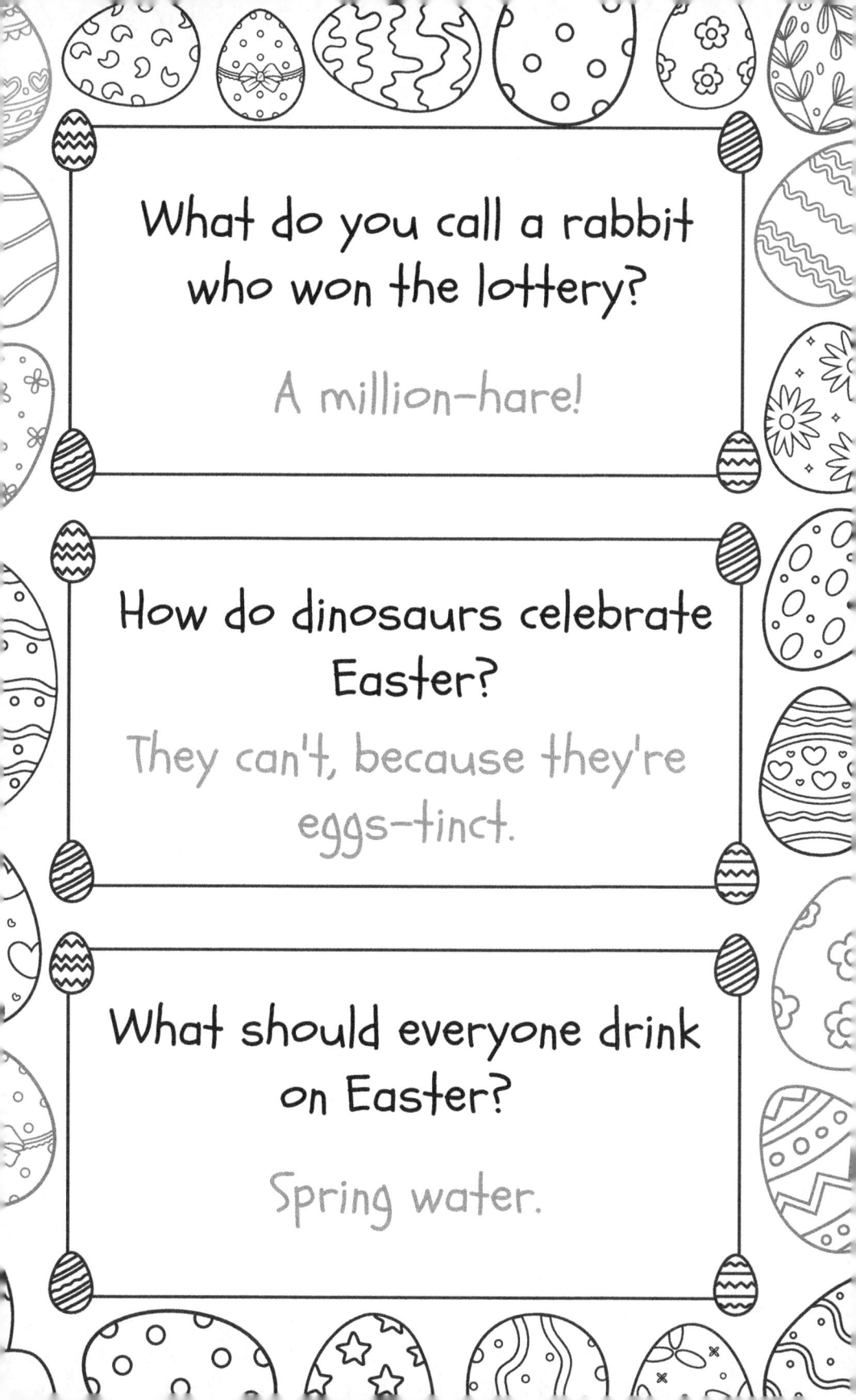

A million-hare!

How do dinosaurs celebrate Easter?

They can't, because they're eggs-tinct.

What should everyone drink on Easter?

Spring water.

How do you get a bunny to work overtime?

Simply raise its celery.

How do chickens leave the building?

They use the eggs-it!

How did the Easter egg win the art show?

He had some egg-straordinary paintings!

Why couldn't the Easter Bunny watch his favorite show?

Because his TV was scrambled!

How does the Easter Bunny keep his fur neat?

Hare spray!

Why did the baby chick cross the road?

To meet up with her Peeps.

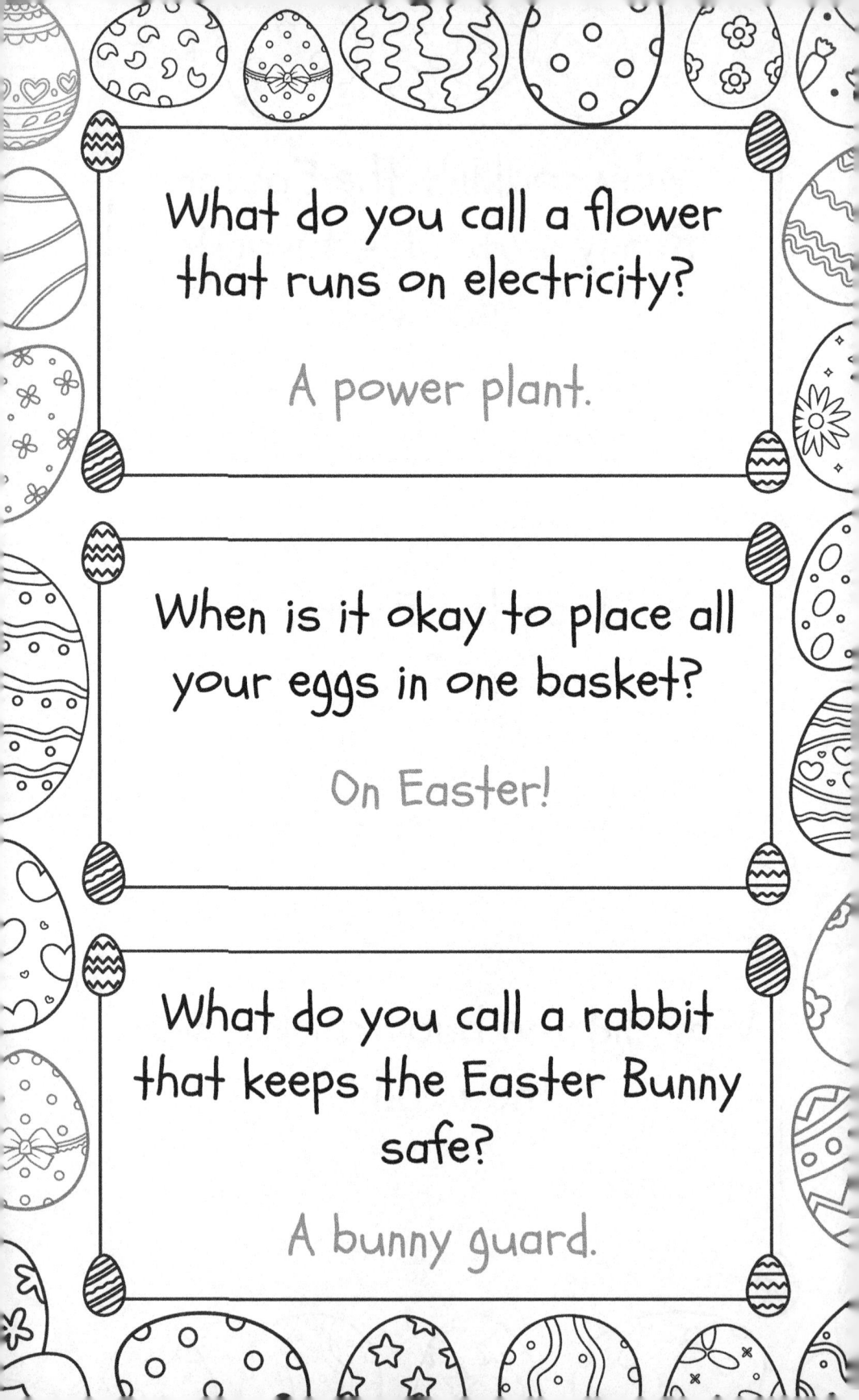

What do you call a flower that runs on electricity?

A power plant.

When is it okay to place all your eggs in one basket?

On Easter!

What do you call a rabbit that keeps the Easter Bunny safe?

A bunny guard.

Knock, knock.
Who's there?
Alpaca.
Alpaca who?
Alpaca basket for the Easter Bunny!

Knock, knock
Who's there?
Egg.
Egg who?
Egg-cited to see you this Easter!

What did the Easter bunny say to its spouse?

You're ear-resistable.

What did the Easter Bunny say after burping?

"Eggs-cuse me!"

How did the Easter Bunny get its job?

It had eggs-perience.

What is the Easter Bunny's coffee order?

Eggs-presso.

Why can't the Easter Bunny's nose be 12 inches long?

Because then it would be a foot!

Why is the Easter Bunny so funny?

He always has a tail to tell!

Why do worms love spring?

Because they dig it!

Why did the bee go to school?

To get a little buzzed on knowledge!

What do you call a bear caught in the rain?

A drizzly bear!

What is the Easter Bunny's favorite song?

"Don't Worry Be Hoppy."

Why did the Easter Bunny keep coming back to brunch?

Because the food was egg-stremely good!

What kind of Bunny can't hop?

A chocolate one!

What's invisible and smells of carrots?

Rabbit farts!

What's a bunny's favorite type of book?

One with a hoppy ending.

What do you call the Easter Bunny the day after Easter?

Eggs-hausted.

Grandma's Surprise Easter Bunny

Grandma wanted to surprise the kids by dressing as the Easter Bunny.

She hopped out, tripped on her own ears, and landed right in the chocolate basket. The kids were thrilled—Grandma, not so much.

Now, she's known as the "Choco-Bunny Incident of 2025."

Why can't we be late on Easter?

Because there are no eggs-cuses!

Why did the chicken make the Easter breakfast?

Because he's an eggs-pert in the kitchen!

Why did the the bunny fall for the chicken?

Because he was eggs-actly her type!

Knock, knock.
Who's there?
Peep.
Peep who?
Peep through the door—it's the Easter Bunny!

Knock, knock
Who's there?
Boo.
Boo who?
Don't cry, it's just an Easter joke!

364 days of the year:

Do NOT eat anything you find on the ground.

Easter:

Go and search in the dirt for candy a strange giant bunny left for you, kids!

Where do you get Easter eggs?

From an eggplant!

What do you call a transformer bunny?

Hop-timus Prime.

Did you hear about the house infested with Easter eggs?

They needed an eggs-terminator!

What's a proper toast at Easter?

Ears to a great Easter!

What do you call the funniest guest at Easter dinner?

The Easter ham.

How does Easter end?

With an "R"!

Where does Easter take place every year?

Where eggs marks the spot!

How can you make Easter preparations go faster?

Use the eggs-press lane!

How does the Easter Bunny leave?

He makes an eggs-it

What do you get if you give an Easter Bunny a pair of socks?

A sock hop!

How does the Easter Bunny stay fit?

Hare-obics.

How do you write a letter to an Easter Bunny?

Use hare-mail!

Knock, knock.
Who's there?
Chuck.
Chuck who?
Chuckolate Easter bunnies are the best!

Knock, knock
Who's there?
Anita.
Anita who?
Anita make more Easter baskets for my friends.

How many eggs can you put in an empty basket?

Only one—after that, it's not empty anymore!

Why do you need an Easter egg hunting license?

Because no poaching is allowed.

Why was the little girl sad after the Easter egg hunt?

Because an egg beater!

How do you know carrots are good for your eyesight?

Have you ever seen a rabbit wearing glasses?

Why does the Easter Bunny have such a good complexion?

He eggs-foliates!

What sport are eggs the best at?

Running!

Why don't chickens play baseball?

Too many fowl balls!

What would you get if you crossed the Easter Bunny with a famous French general?

Napoleon Bunnyparte!

What's the angriest vegetable?

A steamed carrot!

What do you call a dancing chick?

Poultry in motion!

Where's the best place to learn about eggs?

The hen-cyclopedia.

What's the best type of movie about waterfowl?

A duckumentary!

Where do rabbits go after their wedding?

On their bunnymoon.

Where does Dracula keep his Easter candy?

In his Easter casket!

What did the magician say after the rabbit vanished?

Hare today, gone tomorrow.

Knock, knock.
Who's there?
Olive.
Olive who?
Olive Easter candy is mine!

Knock, knock
Who's there?
Bunny.
Bunny who?
Bunny and only you can make Easter fun!

How does a rabbit throw a tantrum?

He gets hopping mad.

What do you call a forgetful rabbit?

A hare-brain.

Why does the rabbit bring toilet paper to the party?

Because he is a party pooper.

Which side of the Easter Bunny has the most fur?

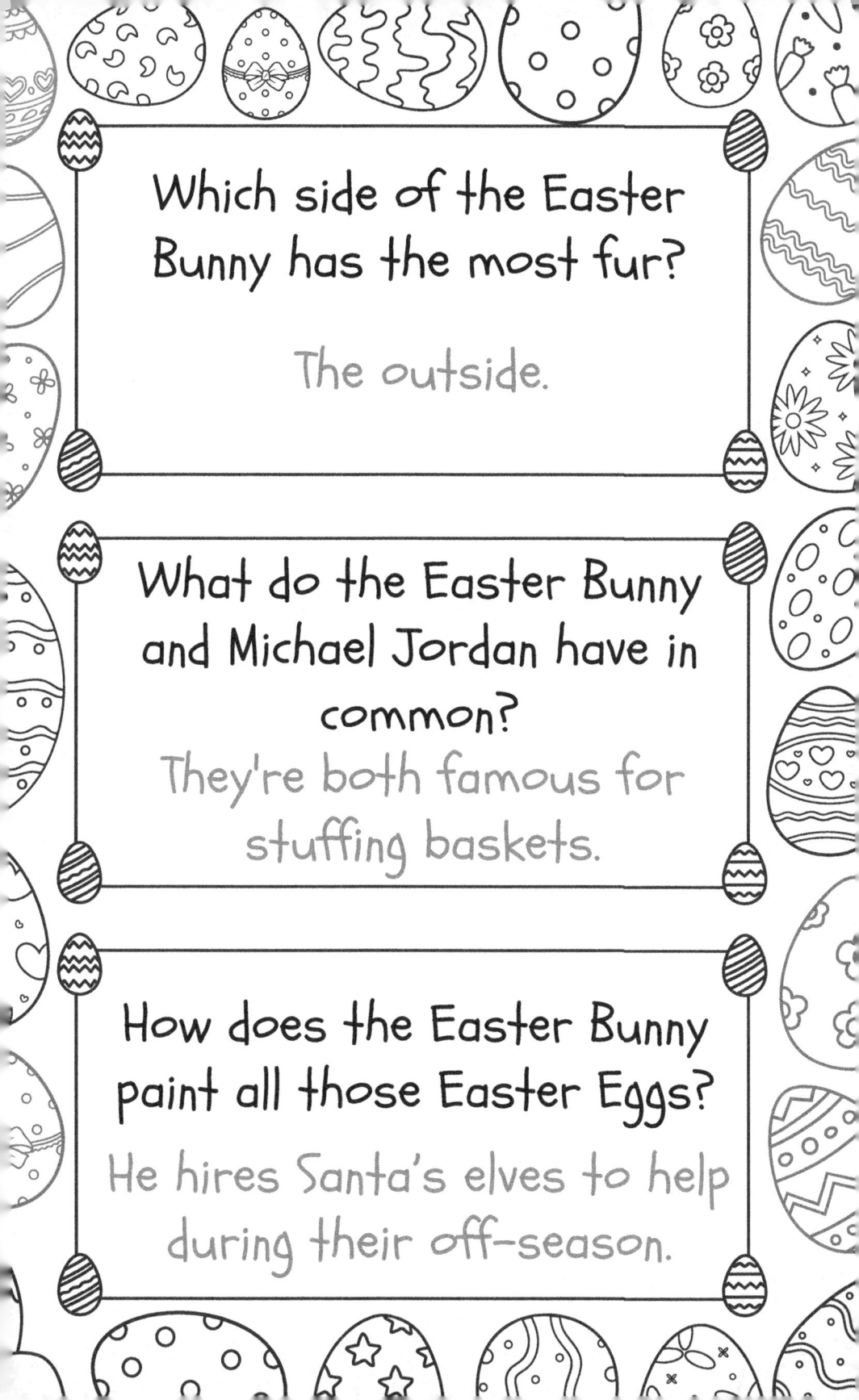

The outside.

What do the Easter Bunny and Michael Jordan have in common?

They're both famous for stuffing baskets.

How does the Easter Bunny paint all those Easter Eggs?

He hires Santa's elves to help during their off-season.

Why is the Easter Bunny so lucky?

Because he has four rabbits' feet!

What do you call a rabbit with the sniffles?

A runny bunny.

Where does Christmas come before Easter?

The dictionary!

What did one Easter egg say to the other?

"Heard any good yolks today?"

Did you hear about the woman who complained about her rabbit stew?

She said there was a hare in her soup.

I was going to tell you a joke about an egg ...

... but it's not all it's cracked up to be.

What happened when the Easter Bunny met the rabbit of his dreams?

They lived hoppily ever after.

Why does Peter Cottontail hop down the bunny trail?

Because he is too young to drive!

Why did the jelly bean go to school?

Because he really wanted to be a Smartie.

What do you call two best friends on Easter?

Two Peeps in a pod!

What did the mama rabbit say to the baby rabbit when she snuck a look at her Easter basket?

No Peep-ing!

Where does the Easter Bunny study medicine?

Johns Hopkins

What is the Easter Bunny's favorite state capital?

Albunny, New York!

Why is spring the most joyful season?

Because it gives everyone a spring in their step!

What kind of garden does a baker have?

A flour garden!

Knock, knock.
Who's there?
Hop.
Hop who?
Hop you have an egg-stra special Easter!

Knock, knock.
Who's there?
Candy.
Candy who?
Candy you believe how many eggs I found?!

What does a cloud wear under his raincoat?

Thunderwear!

Why did the snowman disappear in spring?

Because he was afraid of a meltdown!

Why do birds fly back in spring?

Because they forgot something!

What does the Easter Bunny get for making a basket?

Two points, just like everyone else!

What do you call an Easter Bunny wearing a kilt?

Hopscotch

What do you call a rabbit who works in a bakery?

A yeaster bunny!

What kind of bow can't be tied?

A rainbow!

What does a flower say when it's surprised?

What in carnation?!

What did the dirt say to the rain?

You wash me away!

The Great Easter Egg Hunt Fail

Tom hid the Easter eggs so well that even he couldn't find them.

Three months later, the dog dug one up and proudly presented a half-melted chocolate surprise.

The moral?

Either hide eggs wisely or adopt a dog with a sweet tooth!

Where do eggs go when they visit the USA?

New Yolk!

What is the funniest candy to find in your Easter basket?

A LOL-ipop!

I've got a great Easter joke...

Someone lent it to me!

Knock, knock.
Who's there?
I get Tommy.
I get Tommy who?
I get Tommy aches after eating too much chocolate!

Knock, knock.
Who's there?
Coal.
Coal who?
Coal me when the Easter bunny gets here!

Why is a bear big, brown and hairy?

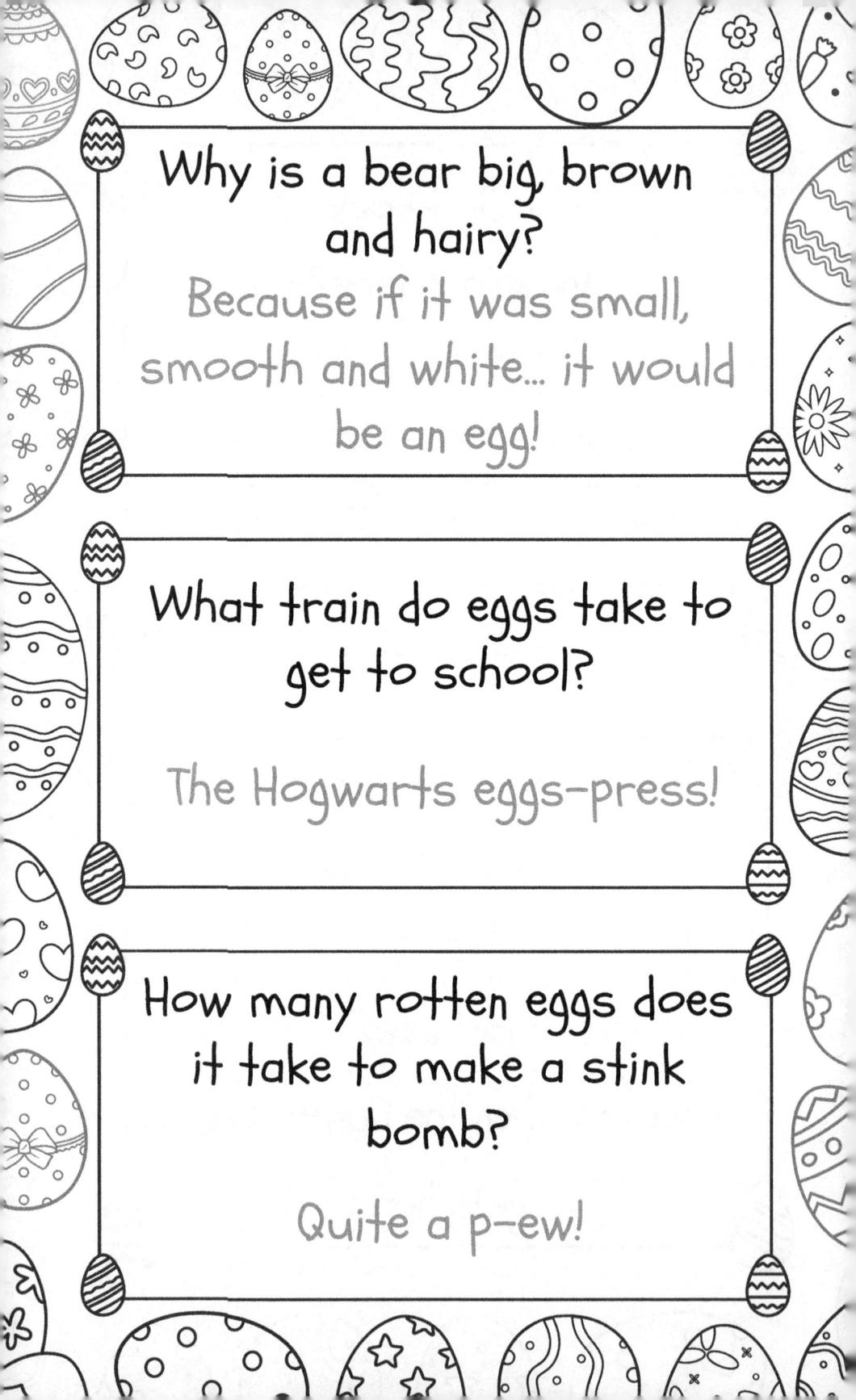

Because if it was small, smooth and white... it would be an egg!

What train do eggs take to get to school?

The Hogwarts eggs-press!

How many rotten eggs does it take to make a stink bomb?

Quite a p-ew!

How do monsters like their eggs?

Terri-fried!

How do clowns like their eggs cooked?

Funny side up!

Who's in charge of Easter?

The Hot Boss Bun!

Hot cross buns are way nicer than cereal

They're so much butter!

Was toasting a hot crossed bun and the power tripped

Must have been a faulty currant!

Where do hot cross buns keep their money?

In a currant account!

Knock, knock!
Who's there?
Police.
Police who?
Police hurry up and decorate your eggs.

Knock, knock!
Who's there?
Sherwood.
Sherwood who?
Sherwood like to have an Easter basket like yours.

Where did the egg go on holiday?

Easter Island!

What's invisible and smells of carrots and chocolate?

The Easter Bunny's farts!

How do you make a rabbit stew?

Make it wait for three hours!

How do you know the Easter Bunny is really smart?

Because he's an egghead.

What has big ears, brings Easter treats, and goes "hippity-BOOM, hippity-BOOM, hippity-BOOM"?

The Easter Elephant.

What do ducks have for lunch?

Soup and quackers!

What's long and stylish and full of cats?

The Easter Purrade!

What's yellow, has long ears, and grows on trees?

The Easter Bunana!

What's big and purple and hugs your Easter basket?

The Easter Barney!

Why are you stuffing all that Easter candy into your mouth?"

"Because it doesn't taste as good if I stuff it in my ears."

'Where did I hide the Egg?'

"I'm always hungry and I love to eat, but you won't find me in the kitchen, take a seat.

Look for me where the ground is green, and you might just find an egg, it's like a dream!

Where did I hide the Egg?

I hid the egg under the

Lawn mower

"I'm cold as ice and have a shiny coat, look for me near the thing that keeps the drinks afloat!"

Where did I hide the Egg?

I hid the egg in the

Refrigerator

"I'm a place where you go to clean up fast, but I'm not the bathroom, that would be aghast!

Look for me where the water flows, and you might just find an egg, who knows?"

Where did I hide the Egg?

I hid the egg in the

Sink

"I'm a place where you go to rest your head, but you won't find me in the bedroom, that's what I said!

Look for me where the pillows lay, and you might just find an egg, hip hip hooray!"

Where did I hide the Egg?

I hid the egg under the

Sofa

"I'm a place where you go to relax and soak, but I'm not the bed, that's a joke!

Look for me where the bubbles fly, and you might just find an egg, oh my!"

Where did I hide the Egg?

I hid the egg in the

Bath tub

I'm at the head of the bed
and I'm soft and snug,

Lay your head on me at
night or give me a hug.

Where did I hide the Egg?

I hid the egg under the

Pillow

I live in the kitchen and can get very hot, if you like boiling eggs then you'll use me a lot.

Where did I hide the Egg?

I hid the egg in the

Pot

Kick up you heels, take a break, it's time for you to be sat.

Looking at me, because I'm the thing, all your furniture is pointed at.

Where did I hide the Egg?

I hid the egg behind the

Television

I live in the kitchen and can get very hot, if you like boiling eggs then you'll use me a lot.

Where did I hide the Egg?

I hid the egg in the

Pot

Easter Egg Hunt

How many did you find?

← Not including this one!

There are:

25

OTHER BOOKS BY
WOMZIZ

ARCADE GAMER

Immerse yourself in 50+ unique designs inspired by iconic gaming moments, perfect for a gamer, ready to color in and doodle any stress away.

FLUFFY AND PLUSHIE ORIGINALS

Enjoy yourself in 50+ unique designs inspired by iconic plush toys. Perfect for a plushie lover, ready to color any stress away.

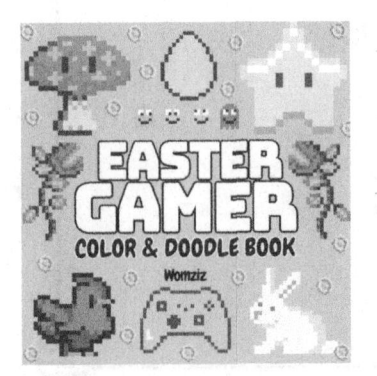

EASTER GAMER

The perfect Easter Basket Stuffer full of 50+ unique designs inspired by iconic gaming moments,! Perfect for a gamer, ready to color in and doodle any stress away this Easter. .

Made in the USA
Las Vegas, NV
15 April 2025